It Must be Halloween
a Halloween Poem

A mom and son creation
for everyone who loves
All Hallows' Eve!

original poem by Kathryn M. Temple

illustrations by Christian A. Temple

For more information, bulk pricing and products go to
http://imbhalloween.blogspot.com/

Manufactured in the United States of America.

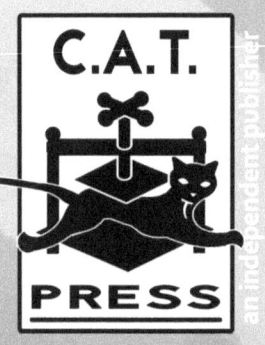

copyright 2015

Second edition. First time in print.

ISBN 978-1508433880

Library of Congress Control Number: 2015904193

CreateSpace Independent Publishing Platform, North Charleston, SC

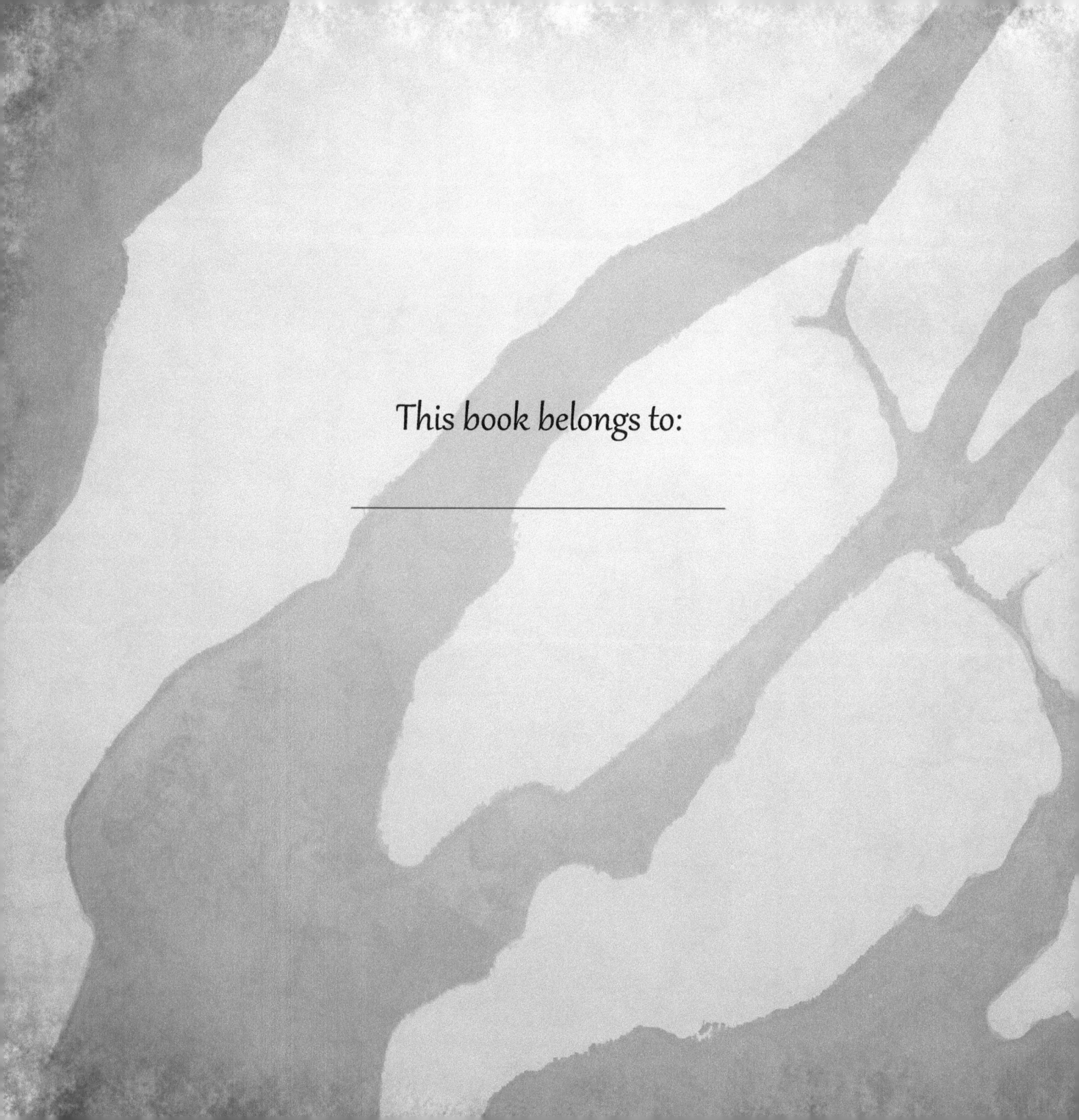

This book belongs to:

_____

An old black cat
on a picket fence.

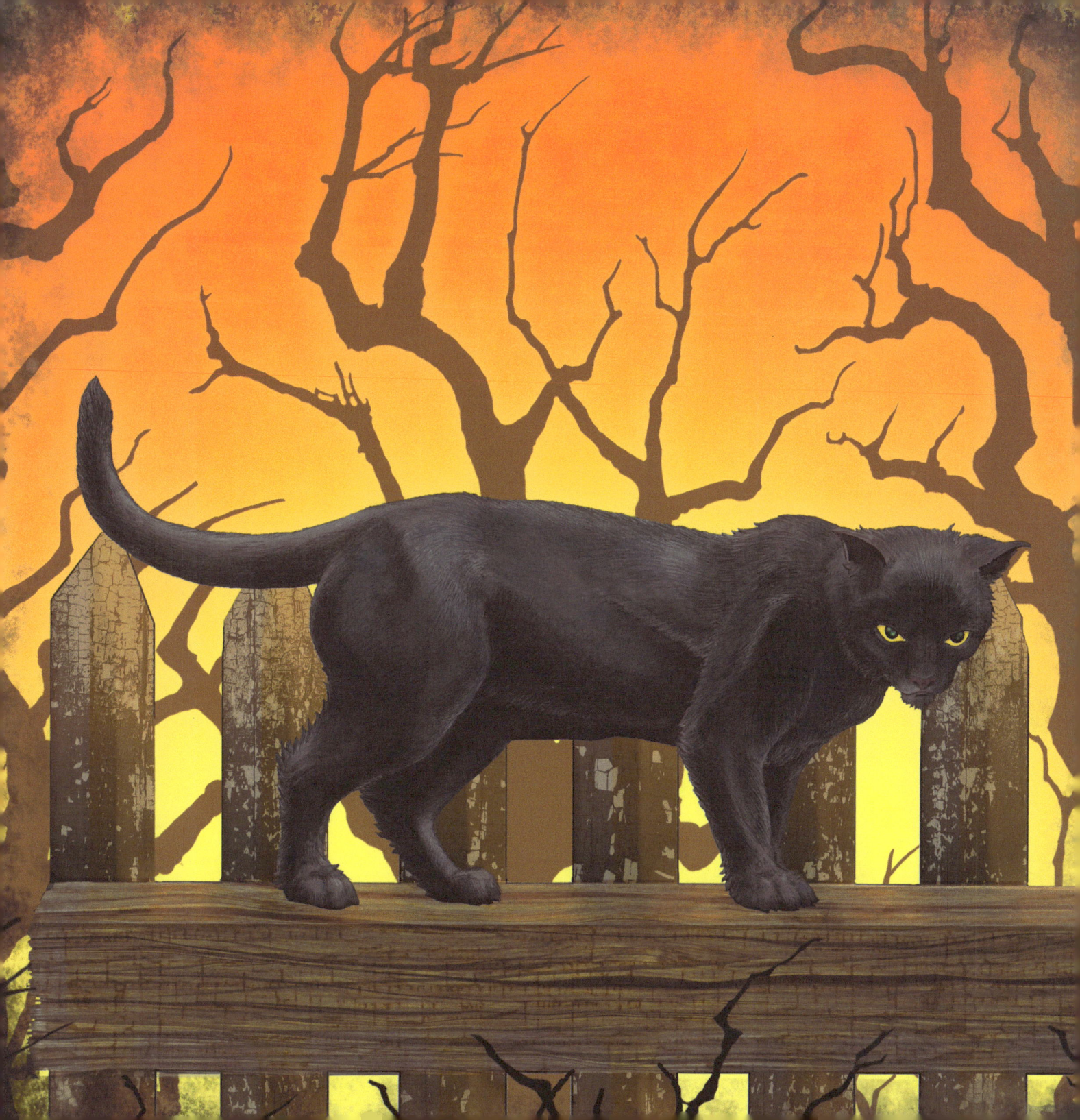

An owl up in a tree.

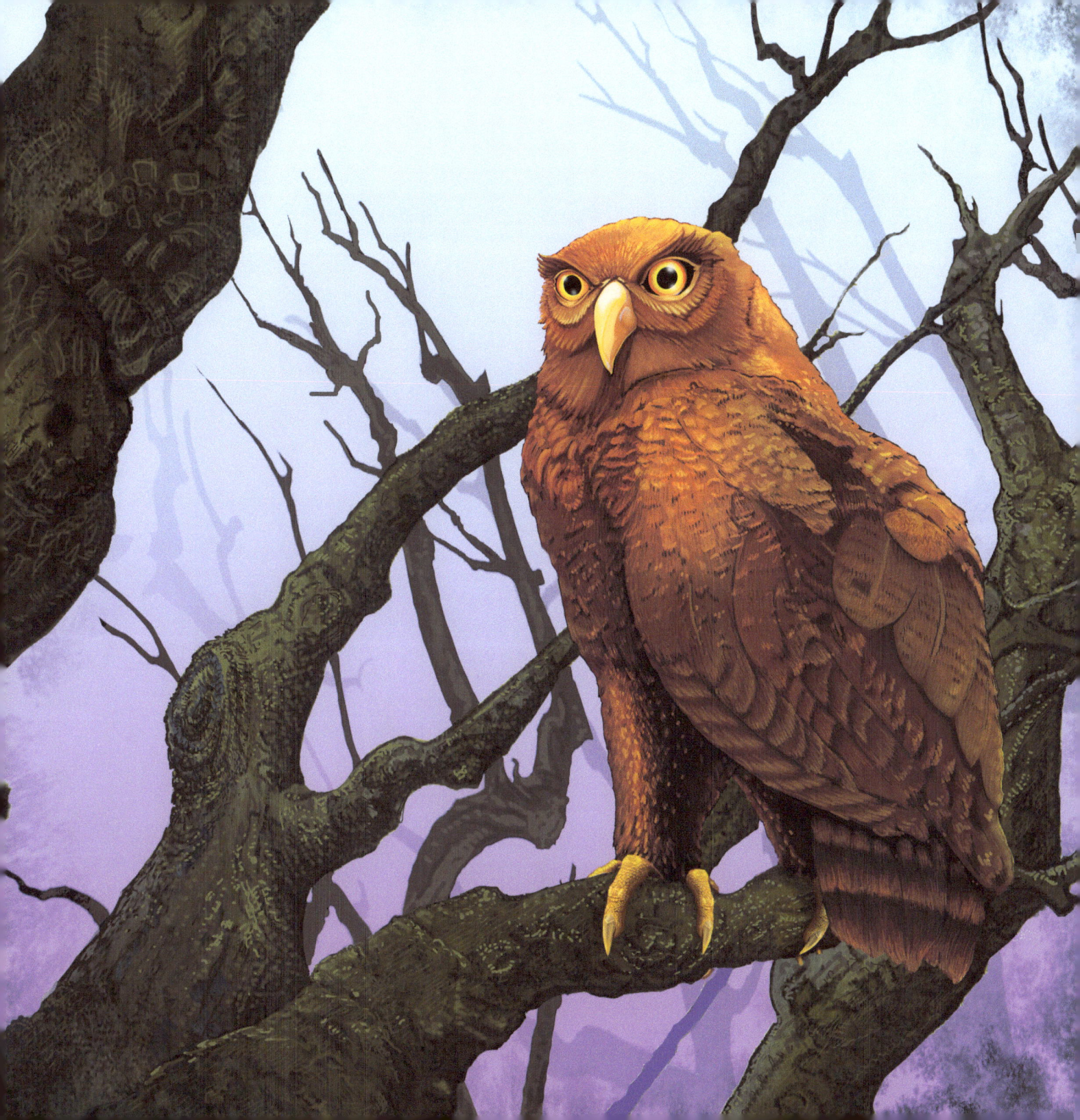

A lone wolf howling at twilight,

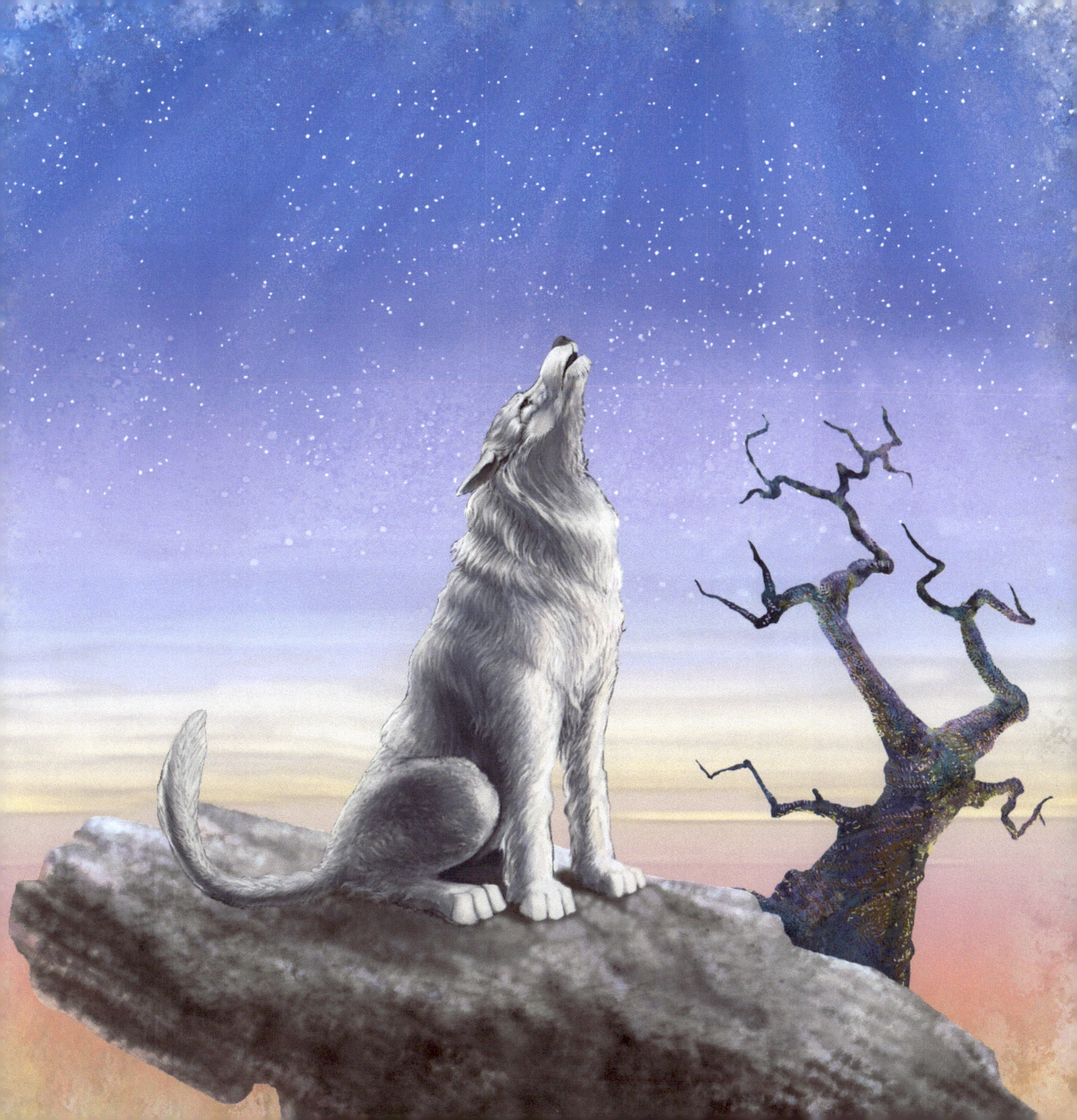

and a jack-o-lantern
smiling at me.

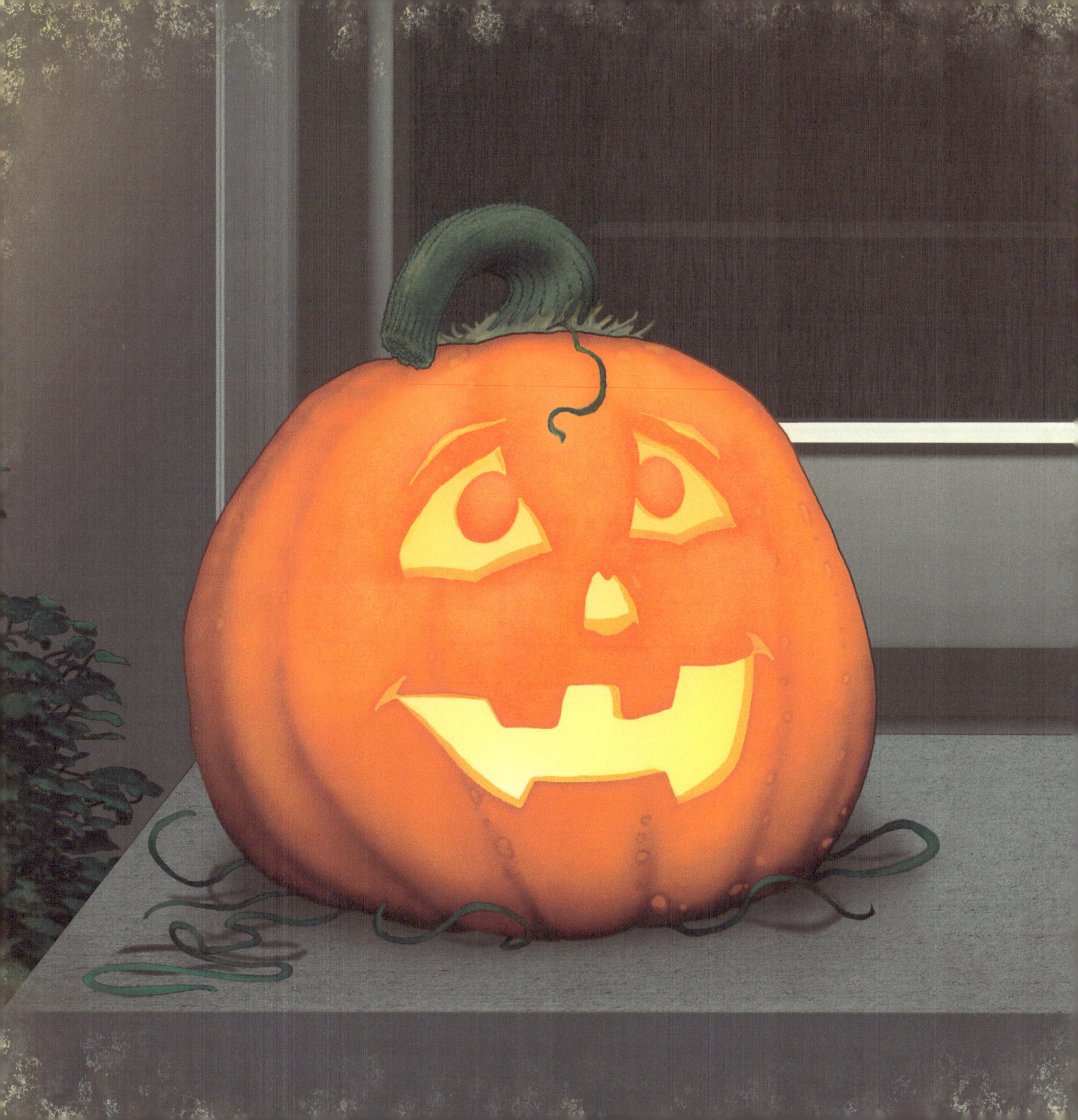

A knock on the door...

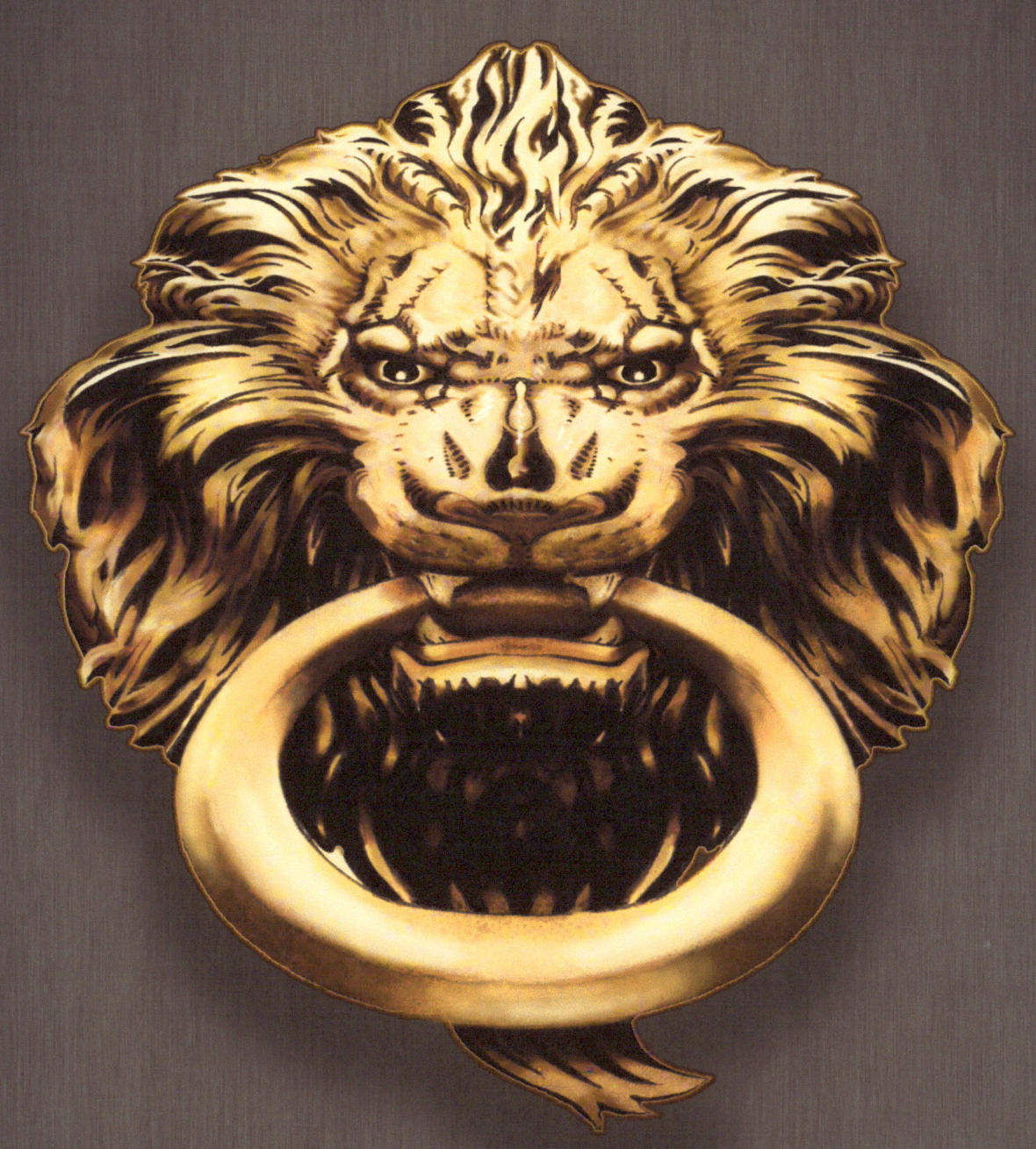

and some goblins appear!

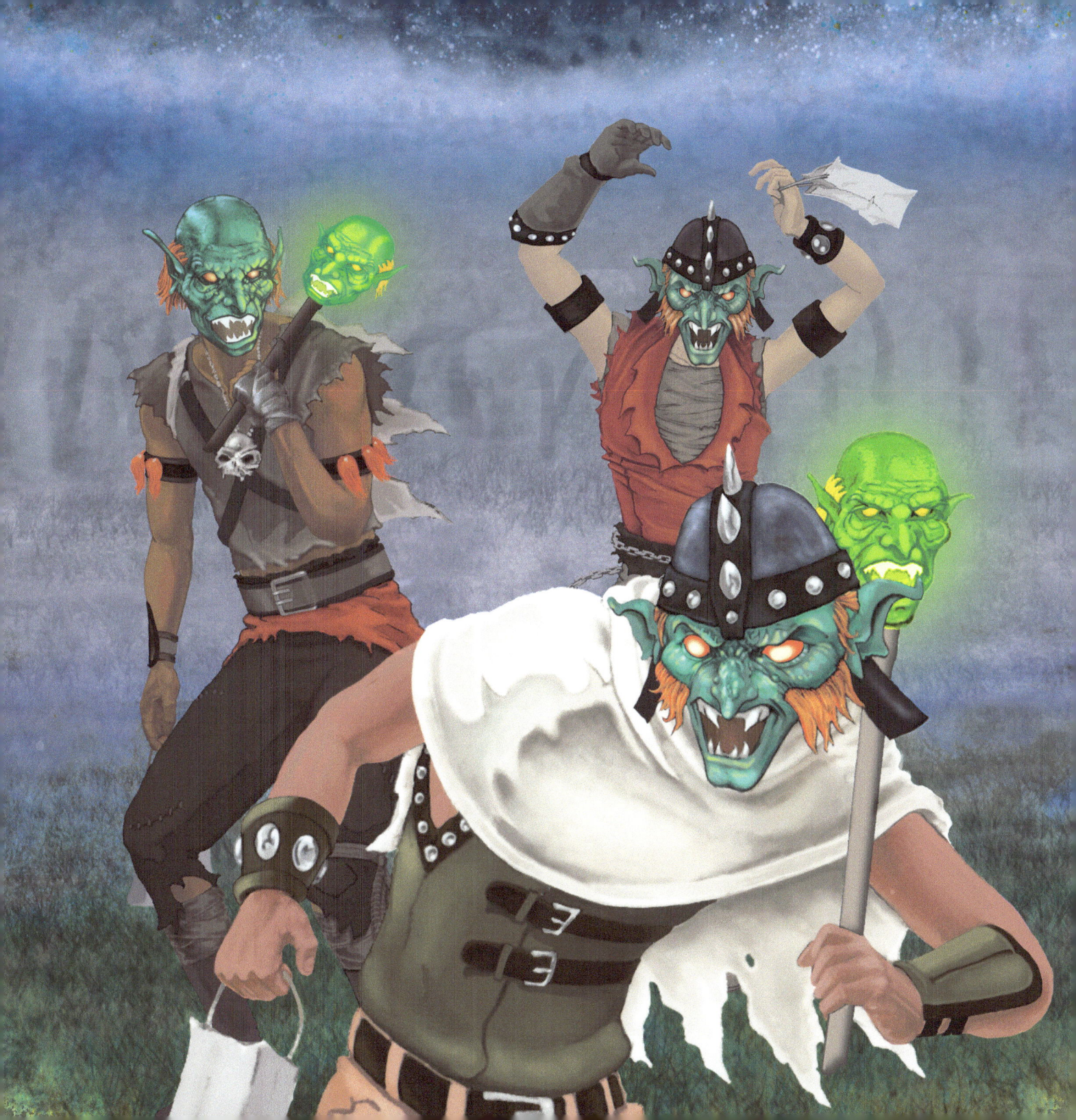

I give them an apple
or two.

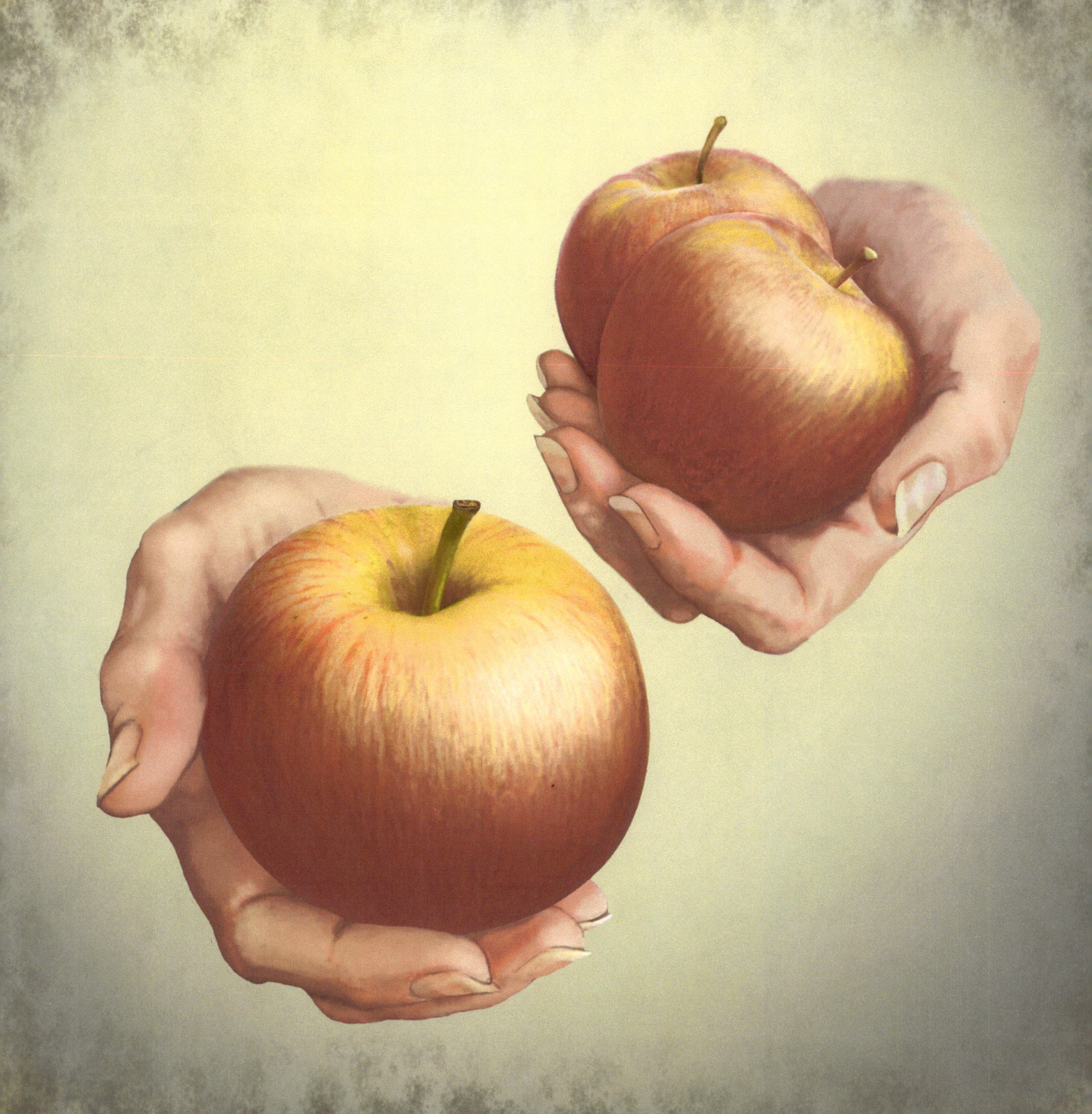

They'll trick-or-treat
on every street
until the evening's through.

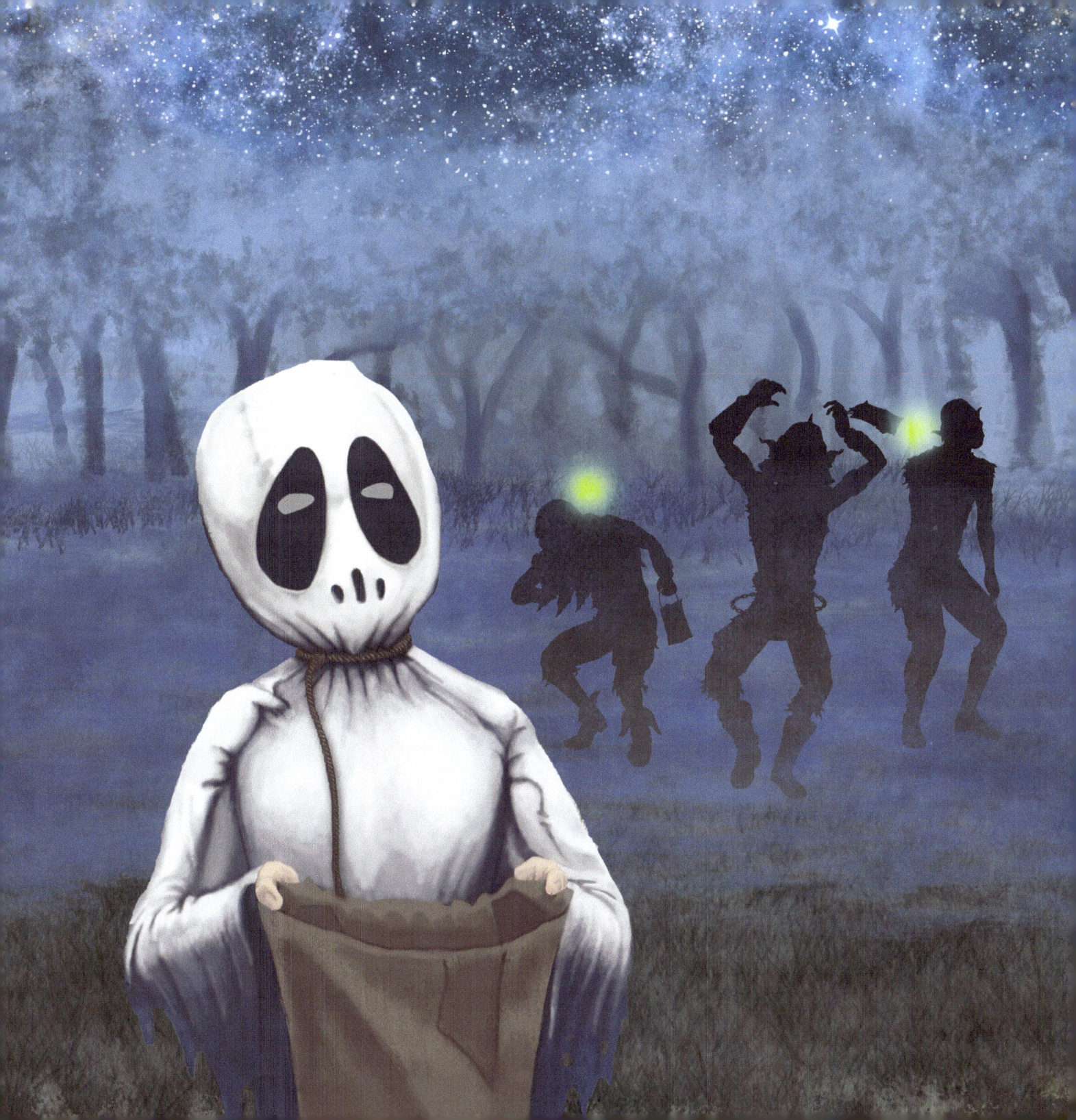

A witch on her broomstick at midnight.

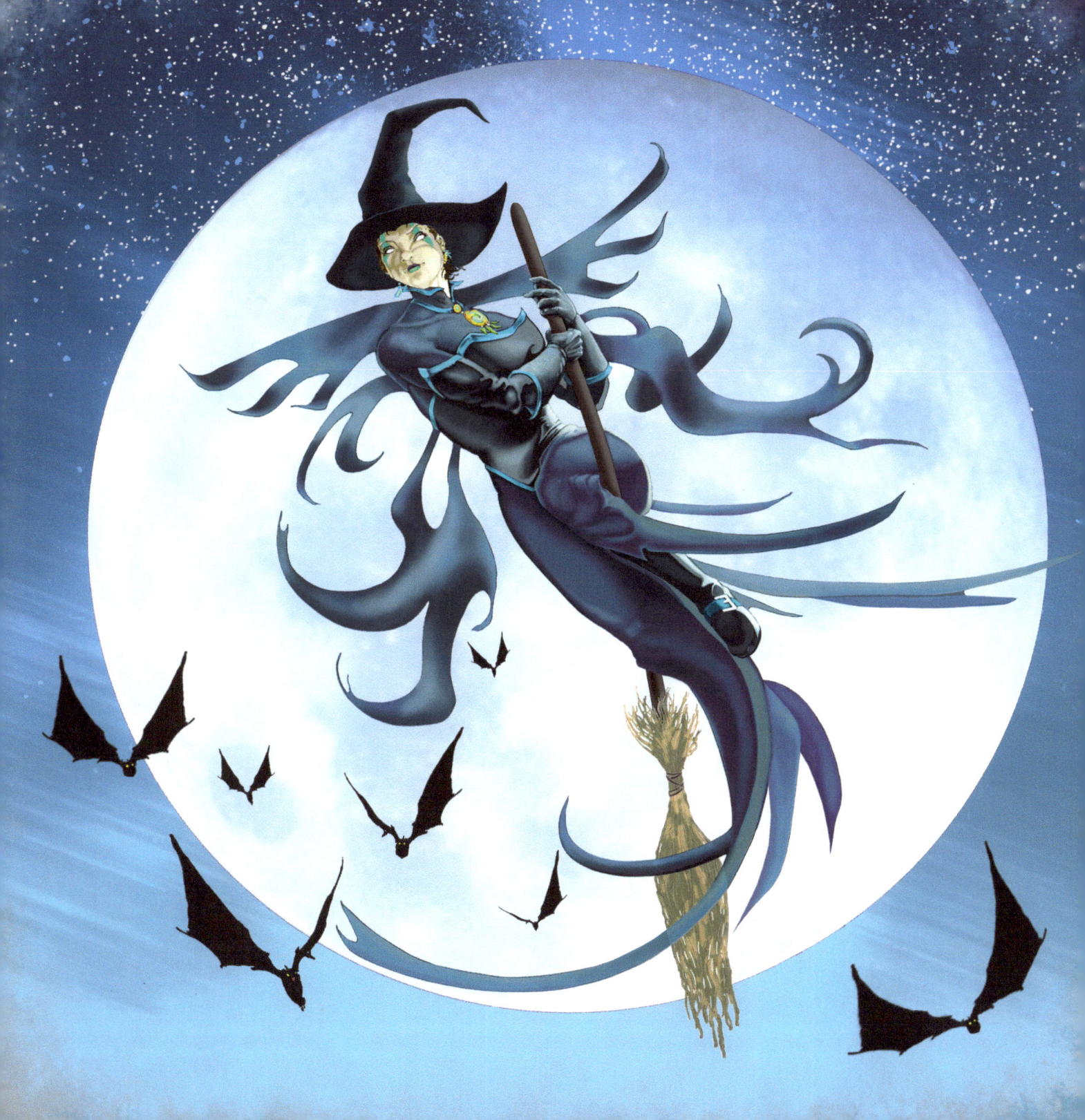

The clock chimes
twelve times,
"cuckoo!"

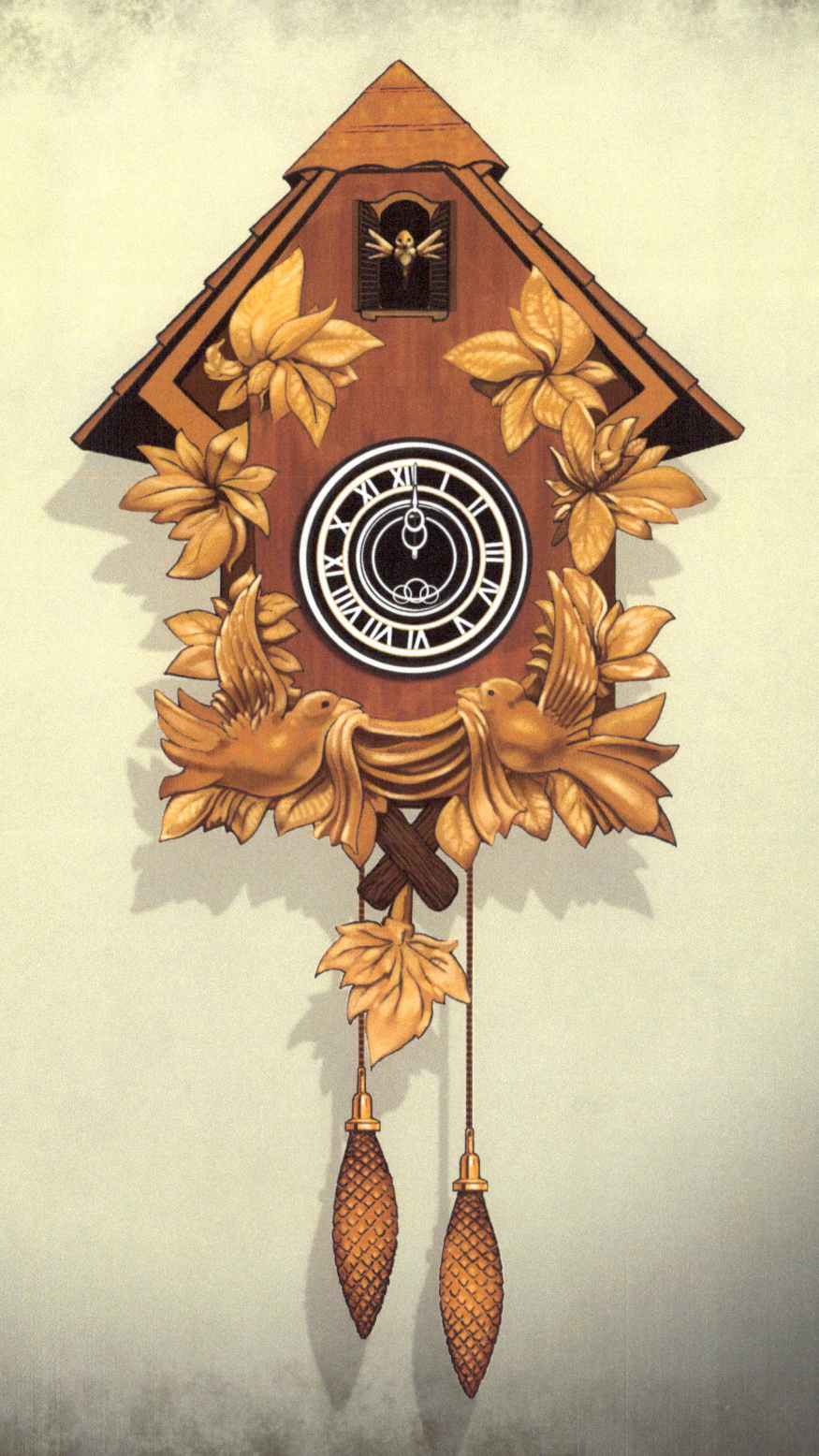

And before you know it,
it's November first...

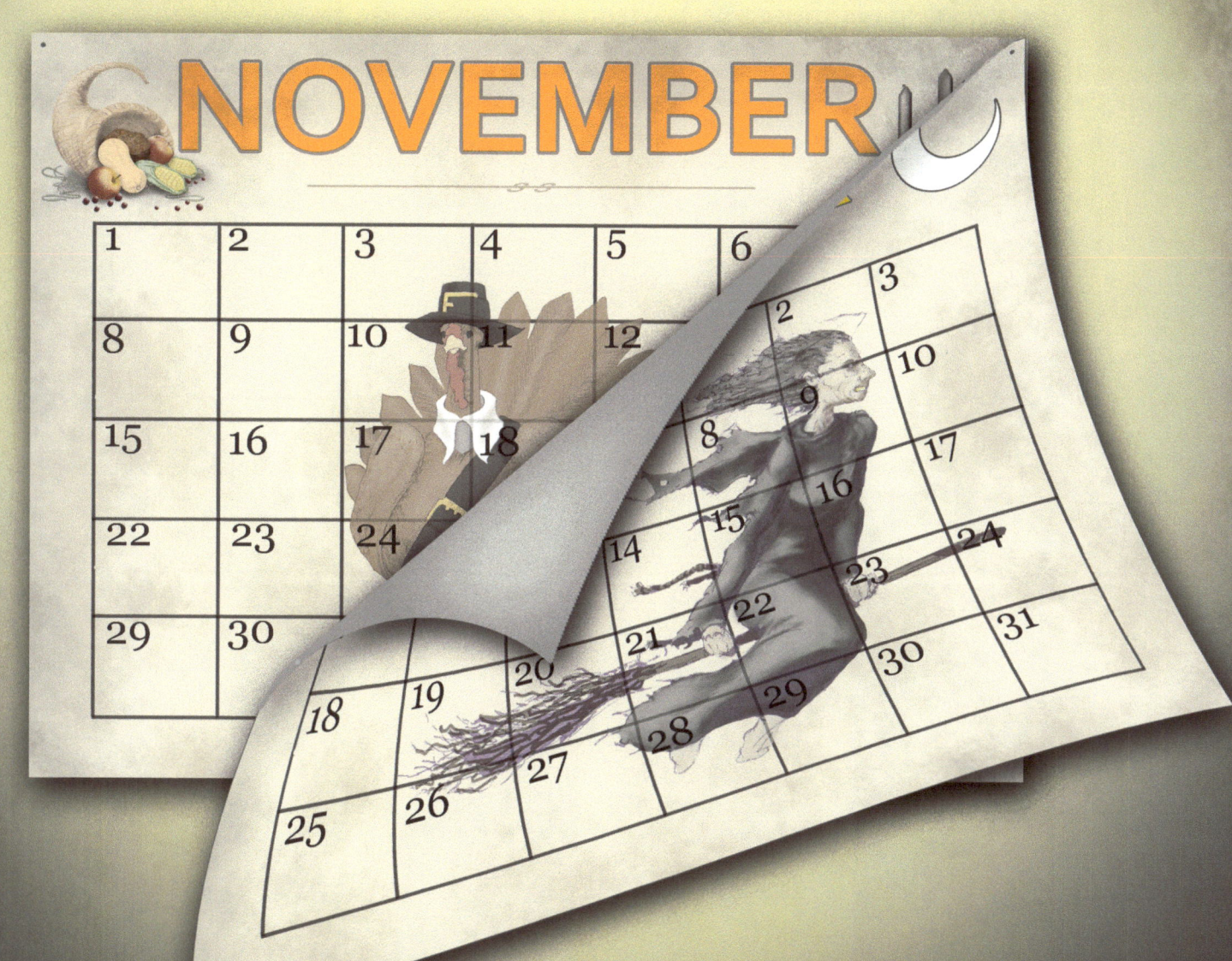

and the goblins
no longer
say, "Boo!"

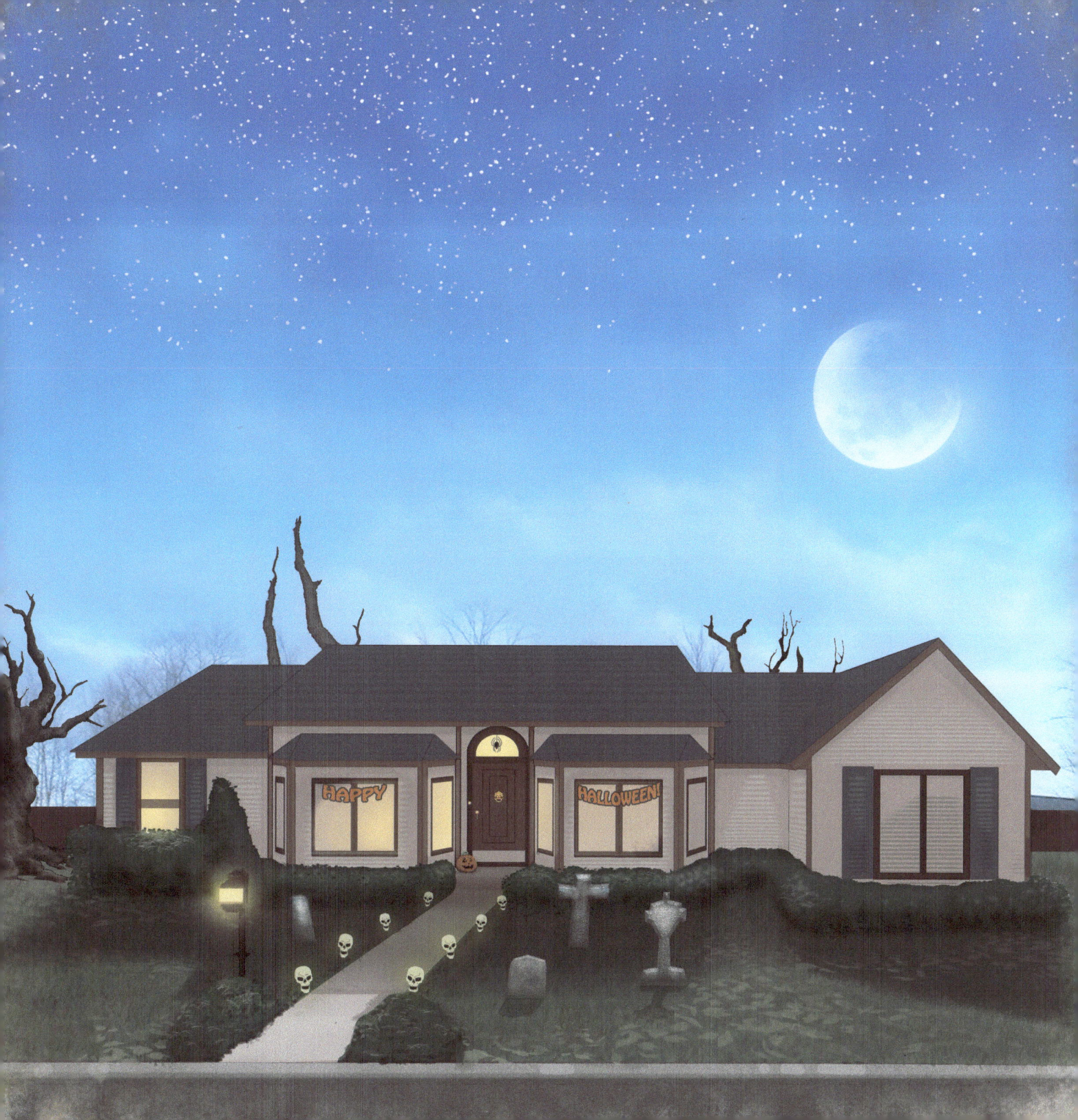

It Must be Halloween
a Halloween Poem

An old black cat on a picket fence.
An owl up in a tree.
A lone wolf howling at twilight,
  and a jack-o-lantern smiling at me.

A knock on the door...
  and some goblins appear!
I give them an apple or two.
They'll trick-or-treat on every street
  until the evening's through.

A witch on her broomstick at midnight.
The clock chimes twelve times, "cuckoo!"
And before you know it, it's November first...
  and the goblins no longer say, "Boo!"

Original Poem

An old black cat on a picket fence.
An owl up in a tree.
A witch on her broom at midnight,
 and a jack-o-lantern smiling at me.

A knock on the door
 and two goblins appear!
I give them an apple or two.
And before you know it,
 it's November first...
 and the goblins
  no longer
   say, "Boo!"

1977 - Kathryn M. Temple
- "for my sons, Donny and Christian"

It was a lot of fun creating our first illustrated book!
We hope you love it as much as we do.

Enjoy the rest of the book
and have fun with it!

Copy and cut out the last few pages
as decorations or for crafts.

Don't try to cut anything
unless there is an adult nearby.

Get an adult to help.
Cut out the jack-o-lantern and hang it up!

This page is blank so you can copy or cut out the other side.

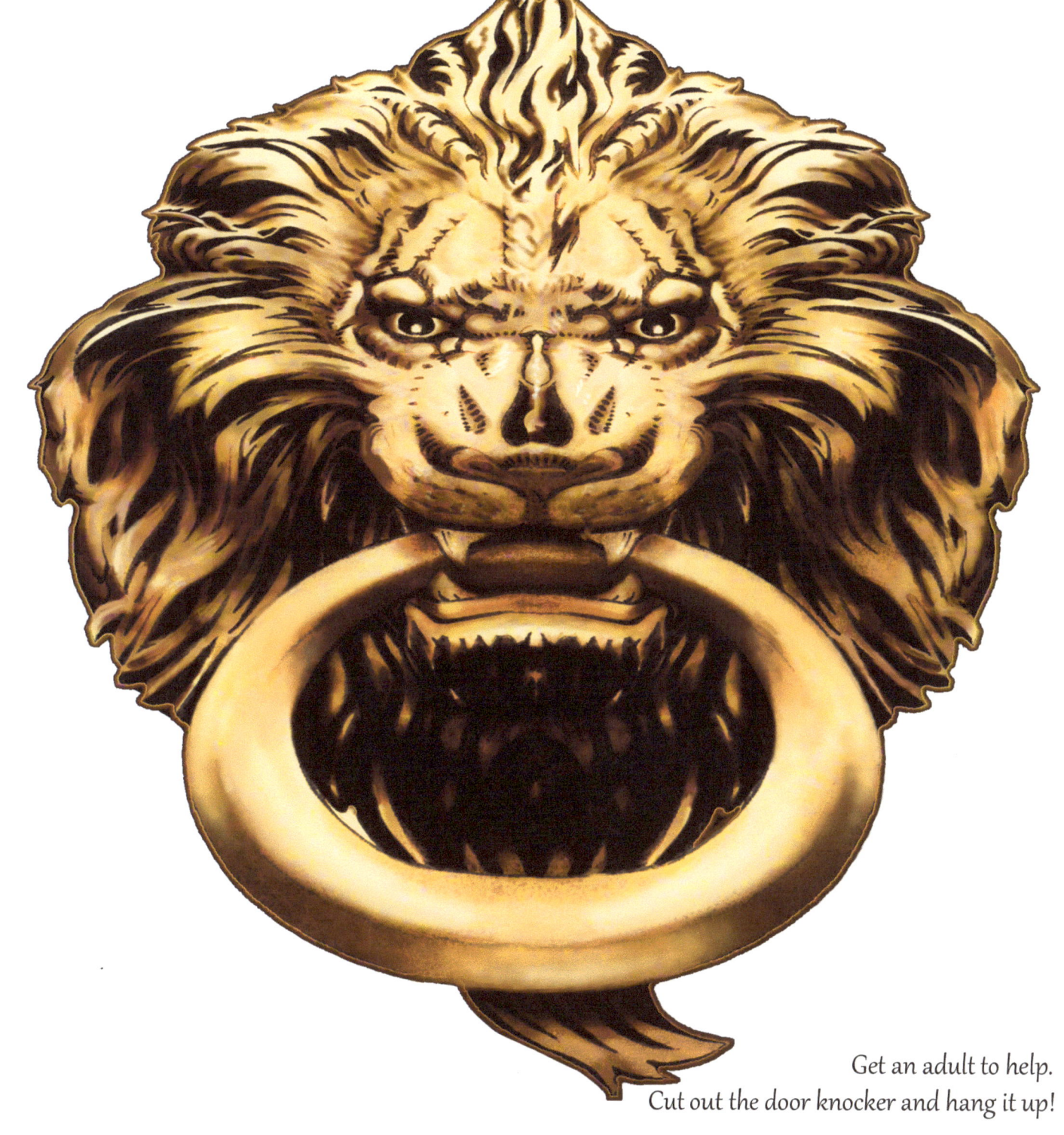

Get an adult to help.
Cut out the door knocker and hang it up!

This page is blank so you can copy or cut out the other side.

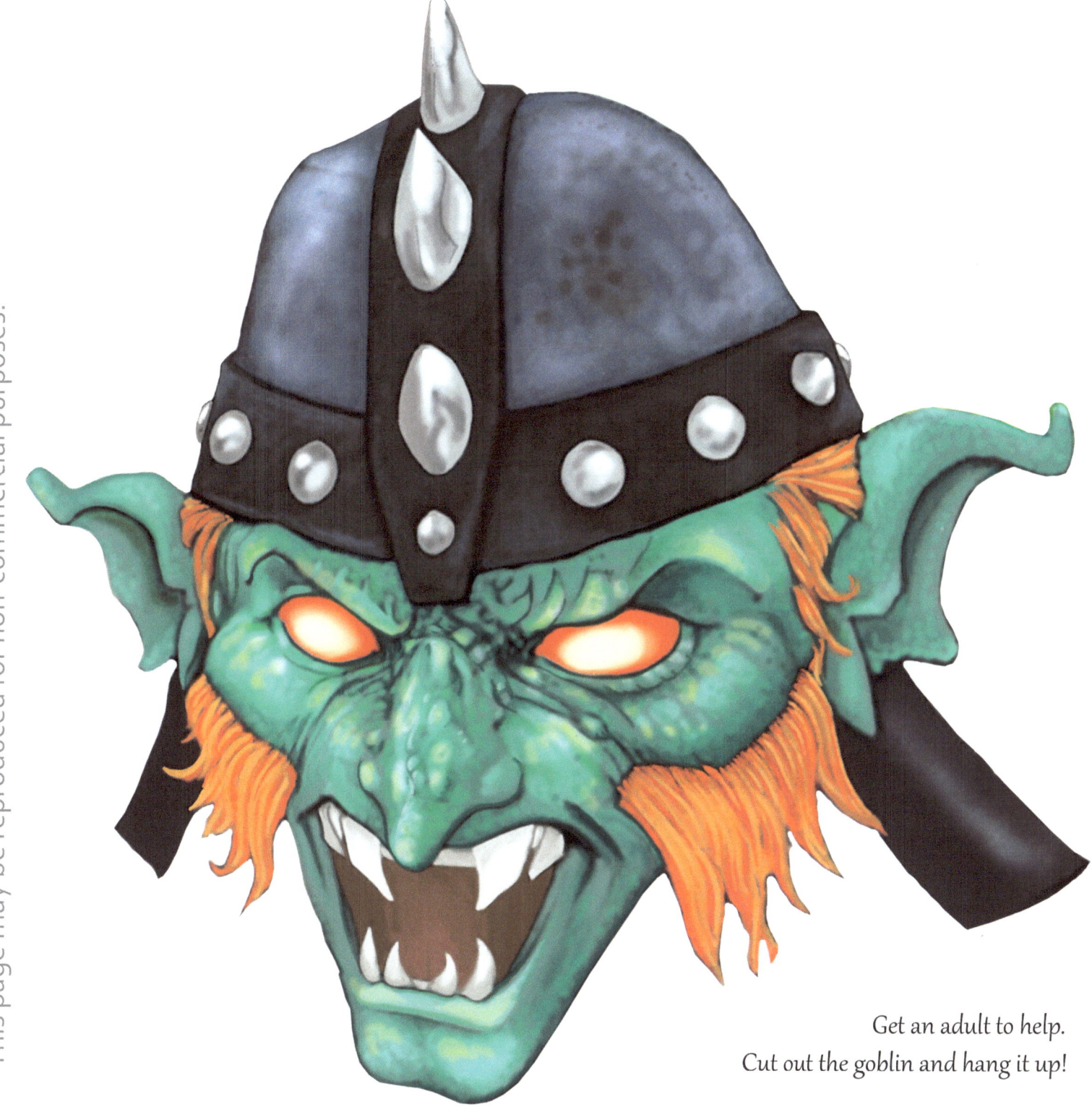

Get an adult to help.
Cut out the goblin and hang it up!

This page is blank so you can copy or cut out the other side.

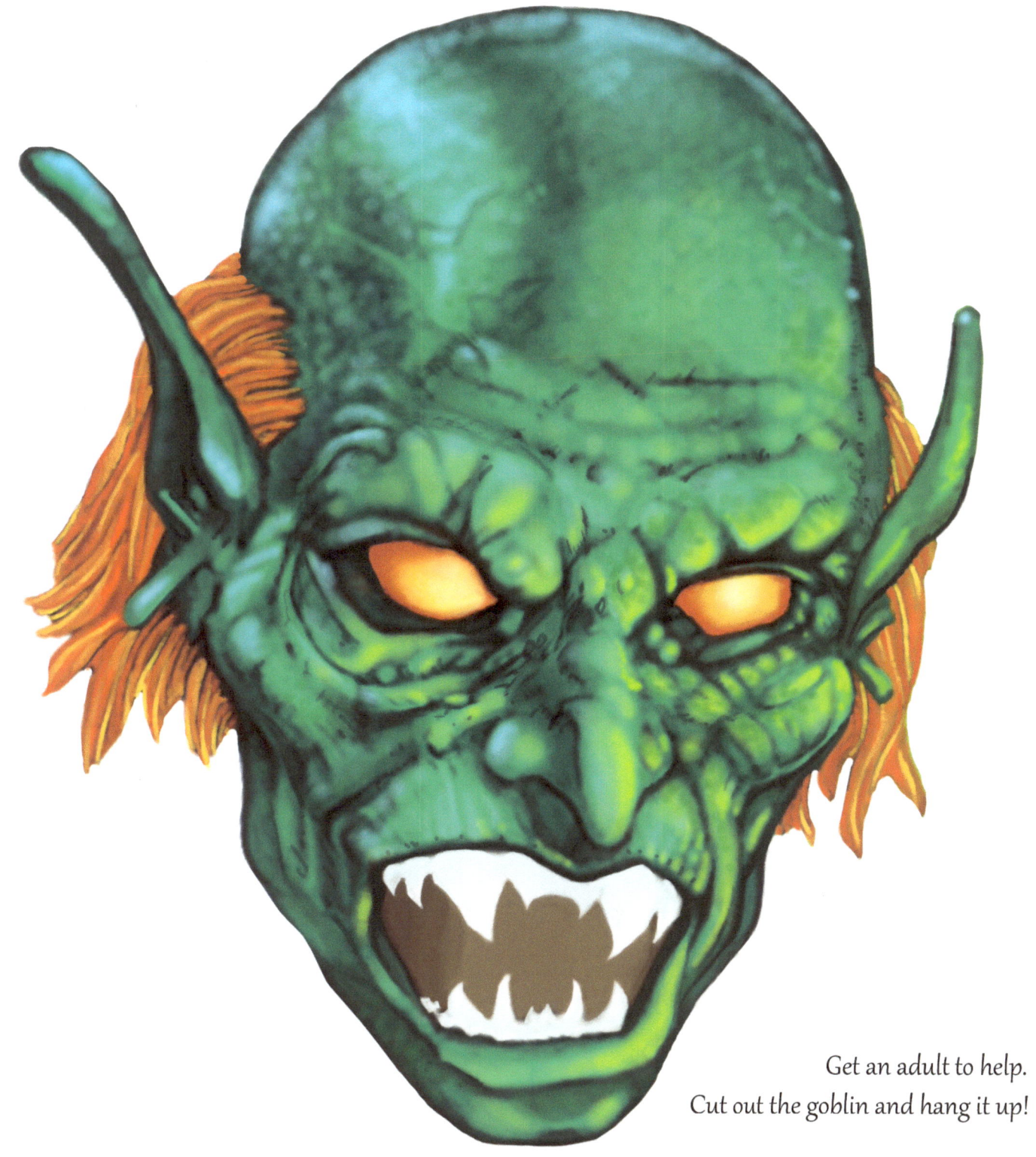

Get an adult to help.
Cut out the goblin and hang it up!

This page is blank so you can copy or cut out the other side.

Get an adult to help.
Cut out the witch and hang her up!

This page is blank so you can copy or cut out the other side.

www.ingramcontent.com/pod-product-compliance
Lightning Source LLC
Chambersburg PA
CBHW050840180526
45159CB00004B/1976